NARENDRA MODI: AN INTERPRETATION

Politics and Governance

NARENDRA MODI: AN INTERPRETATION

Politics and Governance

C.P. Bhambhri

SHIPRA

Rs. 550; US$ 27.50

ISBN: 978-81-7541-817-2

First Published in India in 2015

Narendra Modi: An Interpretation – Politics and Governance

Published by:
SHIPRA PUBLICATIONS
LG 18-19, Pankaj Central Market, Patparganj,
I.P. Ext., Delhi-110092, Tel: 91-11-2223 5152, 2223 6152
E-mail: info@shiprapublication.com
www.shiprapublication.com

Preface

The Ancients with their extremely limited commonsensical understanding of the complexties of natural phenomenon or Laws of physical universe made pronouncements which were handed over to the later generations and these Old Traditions came to be regarded as Hindu Great and Little religious belief systems. The pronouncements of these ancient so called *Rishis* or *Gurus* or *Shankracharyas* or writers of the Vedas were artificially constructed by the British colonizers to convey the idea of Hindu India which was later appropriated by Swami Dayananda, V.D. Savarkar, Dr. K.B. Hedgewar and M.S. Golwalkar and this Vedic-Brahmanical Hindu Religious system, became the ideological pillar of Hindu Rashtravadis in the form of Hindu Rashtriya Swayamsevak Sangh.

Narendra Modi is a product of RSS "*Workshop*" and as a firm believer of the idea that all those born in India are Hindus by religion and the task of this Government to create a feeling of Hinduness and indoctrinate values Vedic-Brahmancial religion in every citizen by vigorous implementation of Hindu Agenda of Education.

The Economic Times, *The Hindustan Times*, and *People's Democracy* deserves due acknowledgement and thanks. Mr. D. Kumar of Shipra Publications has been enthusiastic publisher and deserves thanks.

C.P. Bhambhri
Jawaharlal Nehru University
New Delhi

July 2015

Contents

1

Interpreting Narendra Modi

Narendra Modi is a democratically elected Chief Political Executive of an extremely mighty the state of India. Narendra Modi as Prime Minister is presiding over apparatuses of the state and he has proved on the basis of his performance as Chief Minister of Gujarat state government from 2001 to 2014 that he can effectively and single handedly preside over all the level of political and administrative powers with the sole purpose of achieving goods solely defined by himself. Modi's background as Chief Minister of Gujarat clearly reveals that he manages public and government affairs on the basis of his priorities and he is capable of pursuing his defined goals with determination and vigour. This is Modi's special personality trait. Arun Shourie, an admirer of Modi, publically stated that the new Prime Minister's style of functioning will be of a "quasi-Presidential" type and not of a Prime Minister of a parliamentary democracy, Modi has highly personalized and centralized style of politics becomes clear when on October 4, 2014 while campaigning as Prime Minster during state assembly elections of Maharashtra and Haryana told the assembled crowd of voters "How can a government in Delhi" work with someone who shuts the doors on us...someone who does not have a courage to share a platform with me? Walter Anderson, a very serious student of Sangh Parivar; and an observer of Modi, Chief Minister of Gujarat, observes "Modi is not the collegial leader…." Arun Shourie again publically observed in May 2015, after one year of Modi's leadership that Modi, Amit Shah and Arun Jaitley, they work as a team and …. They have frightened not just the allies but their own group—the extended party etc. On one year anniversary of Modi-in-office, John Elliot, the author of "Implosion: India's Tryst with Reality", observed that Modi: the man who wants his mark to look perfect. "Love is not a word often used for Modi. His autocratic style is said to have upset fellow ministers, MPs of his own party and bureaucrats. He seems to frighten more than inspire…. People are still waiting for his promise of leadership of change to become a reality". The story does not end here. Narendra Modi, the Chief Minister of Gujarat, seems to have frightened his own BJP Prime Minister Atal Bihari Vajpayee, 1998 to 2004, and the telling example of his capacity to checkmate even the Prime Minister of India, is provided by A.P.J. Abdul Kalam, the former President of India, who wanted to visit Gujarat to see for himself the post-Godhra anti-Muslim riots of February to April 2002 where "innocents were killed, families were rendered helpless…" and The then Prime Minister Vajpayee told President Kalam when he wanted to visit riot victims that "PM Atal Bihari Vajpayee has discomfited by my decision. He asked me, "Do you consider going to Gujarat as this time essential". Kalam: "I must go and talk to the people as a President. I consider this my first major task". Vajpayee: "…. there was fear that then Chief Minister Narendra Modi will boycott the trip". Authoritarian personality traits of Modi and his fanatic ideological commitments to the Rashtrya Swayamsevak Sangh's goal of establishing Hindu Rashtra or Hindu nation-state have made the persona of Modi like that of a Messiah determined to implement his goals in this case exercise the state power to establish Hindu Rashtra as defined by the Rashtriya Swayamsevak Sangh. Hence, the essential Modi cannot be understood without very briefly mentoring the ideology and organizational structure of the RSS whose one finished product is Modi. RSS is a workshop which recruits young Hindus and indoctrinates them to act as soldiers to defence of Hindu community and religions which is threatened by non-Indian foreign origin religions like Islam and Christianity. These inhabitants of India whose loyalty and reference point to foreign places of worship and Holiness are not only different for Hindu religious believers whose place of birth is Mother India but they are also source of trouble for Hindus of Bharat. This is the ideological essence of RSS and every recruit to this "military like discipline based organization" is every day exposed to the teaching imparted by higher functioning who are whole time Pracharaks and Narendra Modi himself was RSS Pracharak. Mohan Bhagwat, the RSS Sar Sangh Chalak from 2009, observed on Modi in 2013 that "Modi is the only one who has remained rooted in the Sangh Parivar" and on the basis of these qualifications the RSS Chief Mohan Bhagwat made BJP to declare Modi as Prime Ministerial candidate in September 2013 for the forthcoming Lok Sabha Elections of 2014. V.D. Savarkar (1969) "Hindutva: Who is a Hindu? M.S. Golwalkar, RSS supremo: We or Our nationhood defined (1939) or Mohan Bhagwat's 2009 statement "The problem is Hindus have started thinking about themselves as minorities. Hindus should have an aggressive, nationalistic stance".

This is the central message of RSS beginning with its founder K.B. Hedgewar from 1925 till today that Hindus have to be trained to defend themselves and a para-military type training with heavy dose of ideological Hindutva has to be imparted by RSS Shakhas or local branches. RSS creates fanatic army of cadre to work for the creation of Hindu Rashtra. This fact was reiterated by Mohan Bhagwat in August 2014 that "Hindutva is the identity of India and it has the capacity to swallow other identities. "We just need to restore those capacities". RSS, its all affiliates including BJP, are working over time to create capacity among Hindus by capturing the state power for the implementation of RSS agenda. Modi as Prime Minister, and RSS Pracharak, is committed to the ideology of RSS as recently in August 2014 reiterated with a view to remind BJP-in-Government that "Hindustan is a Hindu Rashtra.... Hindutva is the country's identity (Mohan Bhagwat). If the goal of RSS from 2014 to 2019 is to expand and establish one lakh RSS Shakhs or local units, it is at work. If in July 2012, it has 34, 761 Shakhas, in 2013, 37,125 shakhas and July 2014 it has increase to establish 39, 376 shakhas. The RSS-BJP, joint stock Company managed by Bhagwat and Modi are pursuing its Hindu agenda of:

(a) conversion of non-India religious believers like Muslims or Christians especially poor tribals to Hindu religion nicknamed as "*Ghar Wapsi*, one back to original of Hinduism".

(b) banning cow slaughter because of Hindu beliefs.

(c) Impact education thought institutions like Ekta Vidyalayas and others which makes Hindus proud

> of these glorious past and make them read Hindu classics like Vedas and other books of the past which contain quintessence of all Hindu knowledge.

Go to the past, Hindus had store of knowledge in shastras and it is not surprising that Narendra Modi, a product of RSS workshop, Prime Minister made such statement, "(a) Karna (in the Mahabharat) was not born from his mother's womb. This means genetic science was present at that time. (b) We worship Lord Ganesha. There must have been some plastic surgeon at that time who got an elephant's head on the body of a human being and began the practice of plastic surgery". These and other belief of the followers of Hindu Rashtriya Swayamsevak Sangh raise a larger issue about the scientific methodology for the study of ancient knowledge systems which has existed in ancient times not only in India but also other old societies like that of China or Arabs. First, the ancient knowledge system of India cannot be declared a copyright of so-called Hindu religion. Second multiple and diverse Hindu traditions cannot be homogenized under the umbrella of a monolithic Hinduism because eminent historians have an agreement on the plurality of Hindu religious traditions and Great Hindu Religious Traditions is a myth and not a scientifically arrived at opinion on the nature and essence of Hinduism which is essentially internally highly differentiated and consists of many multiple sects. Hindus are divided into sects even on the basis of regional variations and gods and goddesses and modes of worship are also region-specific which differentiate Hindus of India of continental size and diversity. Hence Hindu religious tradition constructed and imagined by the RSS and its ideologies is a fiction and not a fact based on the essential reality of Hinduisms. Hence, the slogan of RSS that "say with pride that we are Hindus" or treat this country is Hindu India is not based on facts. The question deserves to be raised here is that if the inner reality of Hindu religious tradition is its plurality and multiplicity of traditions, the announcements and pronouncements of Hindu RSS leadership and its ideologies that "we are all Hindus" in India and Hindus in India have to be protected by the believers and practitioners of non-Hindus living in this country, the real RSS agenda of Hinduisation of the whole society deserves to be clinically analysed on the basis of scientific method of inquiry and investigations. The real agenda of Hindu Sangh Parivar and all of its affiliates including BJP is "political" and the goal of Sangh Parivar including the BJP is to politically capture the state power and establish Hindu hegemony over all non-Hindus who should accept that either their ancestors were Hindus or they should be "Converted to Hinduism, the religion of Bharat. The reconversion of Muslims and Christians of India by the Hindu Sangh Parivar affiliates is a logical offshoot of RSS ideology and it deserves to be asserted that the current, "reconversion programmes" of the RSS, under the protective umbrella of the Modi government and the state governments controlled by the BJP are not accidental or aberrations, they are sanctioned by Hindu ideologues and governments controlled by the BJP. Mohan Bhagwat stated in 2015 that "...that all those born in India are Hindus. Whether they accept it or not they are culturally, nationally and DNA wise the same" and following this logic reconversion programmes are, all according to RSS logical because it is "*Ghar Wapsi*", the homecoming to Hindu fold by Muslim and Christians. It is not without reason that the highest organizational centre of authority of RSS, the Akhil Bharatiya Pratinidhi Sabha officially stated that "where is '*Ghar Wapsi*' Campaign, it is just home-coming. The upshot of above narrative is quite clear that it is "Political Hinduism or Hindutva and not ancient great Hindu Religious Traditions which are the subject matter while dealing with the phenomenon of Hindu RSS led movements and governments both at the centre or the state levels, further, interpretations or misinterpretations of the ancient great Hindu religious traditions is not at all relevant while dealing with the phenomenon of RSS's "Political Hinduism" because it is Hinduism in the service of "politics and the goal of RSS and BJP is to make Hindus to occupy "driver's seat" in politics and all the institutions of the state, whether coercive or ideological, should be politically driven and managed by Hindus only. Political Hinduism of RSS is similar to the political Islamic movements in some countries of Muslims majority populations, the most aggressive and violent is the Iraq-Syria Islamic State. John M. Owen in his book of "Political Islam" observes candidly that "Political Islam matters and it is not going to go away soon. It is a powerful ideology and social movement, running deep within and across most Islamic countries today..." Is Political Hinduism in any way different from Political Islam of Islamic countries? The answer is a big no. It is relevant here to mention that many eminent scholars justified and suggested that capitalist globalization beginning with the last decade of Twentieth Century and continuing in the Twenty-first Century will weaken, even demolish, nationalism and a new global world order "without borders or territorial boundaries" would replace and displace the idea of Nationalism. Eric Hobsbawm, an eminent Historian

(1990) observed "... the Owl of Minerva, which brings wisdom (says Hegel) flies out at dusk; it is a good sign that it is now circling sound nations and nationalism". The main arguments of Hobsbawm (1990) is that "Nationalism will be transitory in an era of globalization. How wrong was eminent historian? Hobsbawm never thought that beginning with 1990 is that political nationalism will see a rebirth in a deadly form when "religion" Hindus or Islamic will be appropriated by leaders of movements in India and Arab Countries to fight their political battles against other religious traditions or intra-religious traditions like Hindus versus Muslims in India or Islamic religious political movements confronting Christian America or within the Arab Islamic societies Sunnis versus Shias. Such political religious movements are engaged in a struggle to capture defined "territories for the establishment of Hindu state or purse Islamic states according to Shariah. It is religion in the service of leaders and groups struggling for state power to establish state systems for the implementation of an ideology of Hinduism or Islam as interpreted by them. The challenge to every citizen who accepts the philosophical promises and assumptions of democratic, republican, secular, federalist Constitution of India is to defend it because political Hinduism or practitioners of religion in politics do not accept the basic democratic principle of "equality of every citizen based on the rule of law". M.S. Golwalkar, the author of 'We or Our Nationhood Defined' (1939) and the longest serving Head of the RSS, had clearly opposed the 'federal' feature of Indian Constitution because Hindu ideologies, on the basis of faulty interpretation of Indian history, have always believed and propagated the idea that Hindus suffered defeats and humiliations for more than 1200 years, which they described as Muslim period, not only because Hindu society was fragmented and internally divided, but essentially because India's authority of the state, instead of being located at one centre only, was also divided among various Hindu Rajas and Maharajas. The implication of this kind of flawed history is that India should have "one powerful centre of power" and unitary and not federal idea of governance is acceptable to the RSS leaders. It is not without reason Deen Dayal Upadhayay, an icon of RSS, following in the footsteps of Golwalkars, reemphasised that India needs a unitary and nota federal state system. The Hindu Sangh Parivar has a clear blueprint for the establishment of a highly centralized Hindu state and re-write the existing democratic and federal Constitution of India. It deserves to be mentioned that Atal Bihari Vajpayee (1998 to 2004) appointed a so-called National Constitution Review Commission to undertake a re-examination of the principles and structures of government underlying the Republican Constitution of 1950. The Narendra Modi government is in power at the centre to push forward the agenda of Hindu Rashtravadis as handed over by the RSS. Narendra Modi and RSS are indistinguishable and as Prime Minster he is presiding over the machinery of government which is openly or in a clandestine manner doing everything to strengthen the foundations of Hindu Rashtra where Hindus are "First class-citizens" and Muslim and Christian religious minorities are "second class-citizen". Is it accidental that only Muslims are arrested after every terrorist's attack including Akshardham in Ahmedabad? Is it not a fact that courts have found many arrested Muslims innocent of such terrorist activities? Is not a fact that Muslims and Christians are feeling nervous and insecure under the Hindu state of India? A

French scholar Charlotte Thomas (2015) on the basis of a study formed that "Although formally Muslim citizens have the same rights as their Hindu counterparts, in Ahmedabad and even more in *Jhupura*, their ethnicity disqualifies them from an effective focus of citizenship". The one aspect of inter-religious violent conflicts between Hindus and Muslims lead to death and destruction of property, generally of Muslims, the other reality is every riot pushes minorities to seek collective security among their co-religionists. It is well known fact that the process of Muslim ghettoisation has been increasing because of the feeling of "insecurity" among the Muslims. The Modi Government has not done a bit to assure minorities of India that they are secure and fully protected by his government. It is a misleading statement that lunatic fringe elements affiliated and associated with the Hindu RSS are creating "difficulties" for Muslims and Christians, if so, it was not expected of US President Barack Obama, just after his visit to Delhi on Republic day of 2015 write back to Modi "protect the religious minorities" in your country. The upshot of above narrative is Modi as a Prime Minister or Chief Minister of Gujarat (2001 to 2014) or as Pracharak is committed to carry on his own ideology and belief that India is a Hindu country and political power is an instrument to strengthen the foundations of Hindu Rashtravad as defined and interpreted by the Hindu Sangh Parivar. Mohan Bhagwat has authoritatively opined that "Modi is our man" and this RSS loyalist is the Prime Minister of India. Narendra Modi has behind him the whole RSS 'Machine' of 'organization men' to quote Robert Merton who in a different context talked of 'organization machine' which really matters in a party or an Organization.

The other important agenda of the Modi government is to pursue aggressively the promotion of interests of monopoly capitalist classes of India and further strengthen the links of Indian capitalist classes with monopoly global capitalist system. The monopoly capitalist classes of India and global capitalists are quite satisfied with Modi's performance as an agent of local and foreign capitalism. It deserves to be clearly mentioned here that Indian monopolists are making every effort to integrate with 'finance capital' at a global level when the real centre of global capitalist market system is in deep crises and the best example of global capitalist crises is provided by the "decline" of American super economic and military states beginning with the end of first decade of the twenty first century. It is surprising that Modi's rating by the United States of America is not only very high and positive, Indians are proud of testimonials given to Modi by Barack Obama and the US *Time Magazine* inspite of the fact that American capitalism itself is facing serious challenges. If the US *Time Magazine* has listed Modi in 100 eminent persons of 2015, Barack Obama, US President while writing on Modi in the *Time Magazine* described Modi as "India's reformer-in-Chief". The United States and Barack Obama as Chief Political Executive of the ruling classes is calling on Modi to push forward the process of "deregulation, liberalization, privatization and globalization" of the Indian market so that American investors along with capitalists of European Union and Japan can reap profits from Indian market. It is not only global capitalist classes and their Chief Political Executives are applauding Modi, the Indian monopolist, the real beneficiaries of Modi's free market economic policies have also lived upto project him as the right man for the right job at a right time.

1. Ratan Tata on April 17-2015 while addressing the convocation of Mumbai International School of Business expressed hope "in the inspirational leadership of Modi" because "...the country will move forward in the manner that Modi predicted. Ratan Tata advised leaders of Indian Corporate Houses not to lose "patience"...the country will move forward in the manner that Modi predicated.

2. Infosys N.R. Narayana Murthy on May 20, 2015 asked the capitalist classes "to support Modi" because "we have a PM who is enthusiastic and is working hard....people, all parties and oppositions should rally behind him".

3. On May 27, 2015 the World Bank Chief (President) Jim Yong Kim not only congratulated Modi on the completion of his one year of Prime Ministership also observed that .... One year of visionary steps toward ending poverty in India. The world needs more leaders like you. Are the global and Indian monopoly capitalist building a Louis Bonaparte of mid-nineteenth Century who exercised power over the whole society because he was made of believe that he was above the whole society? A little more needs to be stated here to substantiate the argument that the darling Prime Minister of the ruling classes is not at all interested in solving the problems faced by exploited and suppressed under classes of India. Modi's model of economic development is focused on the prosperity and progress of fractions of the ruling exploiting capitalist classes and agrarian surplus generating fractions of the exploiting strata

of society: (a) Below Poverty Line Indian, Rangarajan on July 6, 2014 observed that if poverty line is calculated on the basis of Rupees 32 in rural areas and Rupees 47 in urban areas "new members mean that 363 million world have struggled to survive if there was no public spending". What has Modi done for these the tore wretched of the East, (b) Gross inequality: A World bank Report "Addressing inequality in South Asia" on January 20, 2015 based on 59 round of NSSO survey, measuring wealth, land, buildings, machinery, financial assets so on observed that "the average net worth of the 10 per cent of the top population in India was 380 times of the bottom 10 percent. This bottom 10 per cent can be catagorised as: "(a) the poor, (b) the vulnerable(people above the poverty line), and (c) the middle classes". Further, the new world wealth estimate in 2014 put Indians 14, 800 who were with multi-millionaires i.e. worth over US$ 10 millions.

4. Agrarian India: The National Sample Survey office on December 20, 2014 mentions that: (a) Nearly 90 percent of Indian farmers have less than 2 hectares of land, (b) An average farmhouse earns less than Rupees 6,500 a month from all sources, (c) The Census of 2011 mentions that agricultural labourers are 144.3 million and cultivators 118.7 million and this huge percentage of rural population earns its living 'exclusively' or 'Partially' working as "labourers" only. Has Modi during his One year of Prime Ministership shows any sensitivity to the

> structural problems of class-based inequalities or rural-urban divide or regional imbalances? Does Modi realize that his tolerant approach for the solution of deep seated class, caste, region division will perpetuate social status quo? Modi has taken great credit for his Yojanas like: (a) Jan Dhan Yojana i.e. financial inclusion, (b) Janashree Bima Yojana, (c) Jan Suraksha Yojana, (d) Atal Pension Yojana. Modi growth model benefits only 20 percent of the privileged strata of society only and proportionally poor 28 to 80 per cent of the population continue to remain at the 'margins' of social hierarchy.

How does one tie together Modi's leadership of Hindutva and Political Economy of globalized Monopoly capitalism? Is it a puzzle that a RSS Swayamsevak and Pracharak can reconcile 'Political Hinduism' with his enthusiastic commitment to the growth of Indian monopoly capitalism? Ram Madhav, BJP General Secretary in an interview on April 12, 2015 observed that "The RSS Chief categorically told our cadres that we are working because of a historic reason—that India needed a major political transformation...". The Hindu Rashtriya Swayamsevak Sangh openly and unambiguously supported Narendra Modi during the Lok Sabha Elections of 2014 so that Prime Minister of India can aggressively push the political agenda of establishing a Hindu Rashtra and a Hindu nation-state because as a committed RSS Pracharak Modi can be trusted to implement the RSS agenda of solidifying the foundation of Hindu Bharat Desh. If this is the political agenda of Modi, he has also to fulfill the expectations of Big Industrial Houses and monopolists who openly championed his candidature for Prime Ministership and the Media controlled by the corporate Houses went out of the way to build the atmosphere for the electoral victory of Modi. The United States based *Forbes* Magazine in 2015 observed that "India is home of the world's 2000 largest and most powerful public companies". Further, Mukesh Ambani's Reliance Industries Limited led the pack of the 56 Indian companies mentioned in the *Forbes* list of 2015. Ambani, Advani, Tatas, Birlas, Bharatis, the leaders of monopoly capitalism supported Modi to win the Lok Sabha elections of 2014. Capitalists have only one agenda that the Chief Political Executive of the Indian state as head of the whole state apparatus should create all conditions which are conducive to the maximisation of profits by the private accumulators. If at the face value it may seem that political agenda of Hinduism as clearly defined by the Hindu RSS may not be able to push forward the agenda of its main allies, the corporate business and industrial houses, because Hinduism as defined by the RSS is a call to 'polarize' and 'divide' society by targeting the minorities to make them the second class states of citizenship which is disruptive of social order in a multi-religious society. Capitalists want social conditions which will facilitate accumulation of private profit and RSS agenda of Hinduisation in socially contentious, disruptive and is bound to lead to social violent conflicts between believers of non-Hindu religions and the forces of Hindutva is who will threaten their religious identity. Modi has to do a tight rope dancing and while dealing with these "two contradictory agendas" he will have to manage affairs of the state by compromising with the principles of democratic governance of this country. Hindutva and multi-cultural and multi-religious democracy in a situation where the leaders and managers of the state are determined to push the Hinduisation of India will definitely lead to contests, conflicts and violence. Hindutva and democracy are in antagonistic contradictions. How can Modi disown his Hindu family of the RSS? Modi also cannot dispense with his deep commitment to build and strengthen capitalism in India. This is the crux of the issue while focusing attention on Prime Minister Narendra Modi.

2

Election Verdict: 2014

A few salient, even exceptional, features of the 16th Lok Sabha electoral verdict of 2014 deserve to be highlighted for understanding the true meaning and significance of unprecedented voters 'turnout of 66.38 per cent. It has been always maintained by important theorists of electoral political Representative democracy that an exceptional voters' turnout happens only when elections are held and voters feel that an extraordinary situation exists in society and because of much a special situation, the voters come out to exercise their right to vote. The first illustration to substantiate this theory of elections is that of the Lok Sabha elections of 1984 when large number of voters rushed towards the polling booths to exercise their right to vote because they all felt that country's security is threatened because even Indira Gandhi, Prime Minister of India, could not be saved from the bullets of the assassins. Post-Indira Gandhi elections took place under extraordinary conditions when people felt that India was under siege and the need of the hour was to elect a formidable government with a clear majority of seats in the Lok Sabha. Is 2014 a repeat story of the post-Indira Gandhi elections of 1984? If a common voter feels that he cannot sit at home, because his "vote" matters, otherwise the existing crisis will further deeper, if a government-in-power is politically weak and vulnerable to all kinds of competing and conflicting pressures. Did Indians feel that the Manmohan Singh at the Centre was not at all equal to face the challenges of 2014 India? Perhaps the voters in 2014 desired an alternative to the Congress-led UPA government because of their perception that is was only a capable and effective governmental and political leadership that could deliver the goods. The Manmohan Singh government for many reasons was perhaps perceived as incapable and weak to perform its responsibilities of proper governance of the country and hence its replacement and displacement have an absolute necessity for the present times. Hence, Narendra Modi-led Bharatiya Janata Party was given a clear mandate and for the first time the party received 282 seats in the Lok Sabha of 543 members.

May be, even BJP has been impressed by its robust electoral victory in its history of fighting nineteen Lok Sabha elections beginning from 1952 to 2014.

Table I: BJP's Performance

The Rise and Fall

Year	*Contested*	*Won*	*Vote Share (in per cent)*	*Votes polled (in crore)*
1989	225	85	11.36	3.42
1991	468	120	20.11	5.53
1996	471	161	20.29	6.79
1998	388	182	25.59	9.43
1999	339	182	23.75	8.66
2004	364	138	22.16	8.64
2009	433	116	18.8	7.84

Source: Indian Express, Delhi, May 19, 2014-06-18

The Table I clearly shows that the Atal Bihari Vajpayee-led coalition government at the Centre could get only 182 Lok Sabha seats in 1996 and 1998 and on the basis of support of a large number of coalition partners, it was able to come to power at the centre in 1996 and 1998. This is BJP's past. Its present is quite different not only because it has majority of 282 seats of its own. L.K. Advani, while presiding over BJP's elected MPs on May 20, 2014, observed that this remarkable electoral victory of the party should be attributed to the single handed successful campaigning by Narendra Modi and only Modi deserves full credit for winning 282 Lok Sabha seats in 2014. If the winning party itself has recognised the pre-eminent status of Modi, any other evidence is not required to state that the whole electoral battle for 2014 was fought around Modi as a leader.

Further, India has a competitive multi polar-party system, it is essential to mention the percentage of votes polled by other important contestants in 2014.

The Table II clearly shows that except the BJP and Congress which polled 31.0 per cent and 19.3 per cent of the total votes polled, all other state level based parties and groups received from 4 per cent to 0.3 per cent of votes polled because of their limited geographical reach and hence support of the voters. Only BJP and Congress are an all-India national parties and all others are limited to particular states of India. If BJP has obtained 282 seats, the Congress (44), the ADMK (37), The Biju Janata Dal (20) and Trinamool Congress (34) and all others have limited number of seats in the 16th Lok Sabha. The picture of Lok Sabha elections cannot become clear without briefly referring to the status of once dominant majority party which ruled over India.

Table II: Final Vote-Shares of Major Palyers—2014

Party	*Vote Share (in %)*
BJP	31
Congress	19.3
BSP	4.1
TMC	3.8
SP	3.4
AIADMK	3.3
CPM	3.2
Independents	3
TDP	2.5
YSRCP	2.5
AAP	2
Shiv Sena	1.9
DMK	1.7
BJD	1.7
NCP	1.6
RJD	1.3
TRS	1.2
JD(U)	1.1
CPI	0.8
JD(S)	0.7

Source: *Indian Express*, Delhi, May 19-2014

The once formidable Congress is lying in a shambles with 44 seats and a little more than 19 per cent of the retained votes.

The Table III gives a glimpse of the given situation in which Congress has fallen from high pedestal to an extremely miserable political status.

Indian Elections are very special because on the basis of 'Registered' and 'Non-registered' categories defined by the Election Commission of India, the present day India has 1,687 parties 'Registered' for the Lok Sabha elections. It does not mean that all Registered or Unregistered parties

Table III: Congress-performance

Elections	*Winning Party*	*Seats Won*	*Total Seats*	*Vote Share*
1957	Congress	371	494	47.8
1962	Congress	361	494	44.7
1967	Congress	283	520	40.8
1971	Congress	352	518	43.7
1977	Janata Party	154	542	34.5
1980	Congress	353	529	42.7
1984-85	Congress	414	541	48.1
2014	Congress	44	543	19.3

Source: Indian Express, New Delhi, May 18, 2014

actually contest the elections, for example, in 2014, 53 parties actually contested and not to be left behind the contestant candidates, many frivolous and absentee, 5000 contested 2014 elections. If BJP has recorded slow and steadily growth, Congress has shown ups and downs during the last sixteen Lok Sabha Elections.

The Table IV clearly shows that Congress has always shown a capacity to revive and reinvent itself. The future will show whether Congress is able to really face the new challenge before itself or remain a pale shadow of its former self.

To conclude the discussion about the meanings of verdict, Modi's contribution deserves to be highlighted. Modi addressed 440 rallies including185 Vijay Bharat elector rallies. Modi always appropriated Hindu popular symbols like launching his election campaign after offering prayers at Vaishno Devi Temple with Mata's blessings and addressed his own election rally at Varanasi with a slogan "Holy Ganga Ma has asked" him to come to Varanasi to contest the elections. Hindutva was always his shield and public face. This is an election victory of Modi only.

Table IV: Congress Decline in various States

Congress in power at state level	*States*	*Number of Seats (All India = 543 Seats)*
Congress has not been in power at state level in 25 years	West Bengal, Tamilnadu, Uttar Pradesh, Bihar, Sikkim, Tripura, Nagaland	205
Congress has not been in power at state level for more than 10 years	Gujarat, Odisha, Madhya Pradesh, Chhattisgarh,	87
Less likely that congress will be able to win power in state without an ally	Andhra Pradesh (Telangana and Seemandhara, (Delhi, Jammu & Kashmir, Maharashtra, Jharkhand)	117
Congress still within striking distance of power at state level	Punjab, Himachal, Haryana, Kerala, Karnataka, Assam, Goa, Rajasthan, Northeastern States, Union Territories	134

Congress Performance in Key Elections Since 1977

Lok Sabha Election Year	*Seats Contested*	*Won*	*Number of Seats Fofeited Deposit*	*Vote Share (in %)*
1977	492	154	18	34.5
1989	510	197	5	39.5
1996	529	140	127	28.8
1999	453	114	88	28.3
2009	440	206	71	28.6
2014	464	44	178*	19.3

*Provisional

Source: Indian Express, *Delhi, May 20, 2014.*

Modi Government and Opposition's Role: Focus must Shift to India's Inclusiveness and Diversity

The Narendra Modi model of governance can be analysed only if his personality traits and ideological worldview are scrutinised for an understanding of a leader of a party that has won 282 of the 543 Lok Sabha seats, and 31 per cent votes in a turnout of 66.4 per cent.

It is only after Jawaharlal Nehru, Indira Gandhi and Rajiv Gandhi that a party and its leader have a clear mandate to govern India from 2014 to 2019.

Who is Narendra Modi?

First, Modi is a product of the Hindu seminary of the RSS. The ideological foundation of the RSS is to work for the welfare of Hindu Bharat Mata that has supposedly been under siege from non-Hindu or Muslim invaders. Modi has said, "I am a Hindu, I am a nationalist and I am a patriot."

Second, as chief minister of Gujarat for over 10 years, he ran a government in which Muslims never found any representation. Not was there any Muslim candidate in the state polls of 2012.

Third, his style of governance was authoritarian, by empowering a bureaucracy loyal only to him. He did not appoint a Lokayukta for nine years, till he got a person who was loyal to him.

So, it is imperative to identify some important constitutional checks and balances that can keep the Modi administration within the constitutional "basic structure of India".

First, socially and spatially, the verdict of 2014 elections shows that in spite of 282 seats won by the BJP, its real support base is limited in terms of territorial dispersal among the 29 states and seven Union territories of India.

Even without Muslim votes, the BJP's geographical reach is concentrated in the eight states of Uttar Pradesh, Madhya

Pradesh, Gujarat, Rajasthan, Bihar, Karnataka, Chhattisgarh and Maharashtra from where it has won 211 seats out of 282, and secured 11.7 crore, or two-thirds, of 17.2 crore voters.

But it does not represent the continental diversity of India and important "peripheries" like Assam, Meghalaya, Manipur, Mizoram, Nagaland, Tripura, Arunachal Pradesh and Sikkim on the one hand, and Jammu and Kashmir on the other.

Arunachal Pradesh has a Congress-led government, Tripura has a Left-led government, and even in 2014, Manipur has elected two Congress MPs and Mizoram's only one. In Assam, Tarun Gogoi's Congress-led government watched as Modi's campaign split votes between Hindus and Muslims.

How will the Centre now help Assam maintain law and order in the volatile region? In its euphoria, the BJP should not forget that the aspirations of the northeast and J&K are complex, volatile and different from the Hindi mainland.

The RSS' idea of India is less nuanced with a more centralised government with a powerful, authoritarian figure at the helm. Centralising forces are diluted when we have checks and balances of a coalition government. But the BJP doesn't need the NDA any more. An alternative political alliance of opposition parties in the Lok Sabha seems to be a possibility.

Only a viable and effective opposition in the Lok Sabha can act as a real countervailing force to Modi's centralisation. The Congress party and its UPA allies with 66 members, Trinamool Congress with 34, AIADMK with 37 members,

Biju Janata Dal with 20, SP with five and a few others can emerge as a compact opposition in the Lok Sabha.

In the first Lok Sabha, the Nehru-led Congress had a majority, but the combined opposition of communists and socialists acted as a vigilant watchdog of people's interests. Naveen Patnaik gave marching orders to the BJP after the anti-Christian Kandhamal riots.

Mamata Banerjee with J. Jayalalithaa and Patnaik floated the idea of a federal opposition front before the Lok Sabha elections. The rationale for such an idea has assumed some significance in the changed political landscape.

The BJP is committed to the idea of a separate Gorkhaland from Bengal, which should bother Mamata. Modi had announced that he would take chief ministers on board while framing important national policies.

Will Mamata agree with Modi's formulation that Muslim Bangladeshis should be commanded to leave and Hindu Bangladeshis could continue to reside in the border areas of West Bengal and Assam? For the regional parties, anti-Congressism is dead and the focus must shift to maintaining India's inclusiveness and diversity.

The Economic Times, 10 June, 2014

3

Lack of Ideology Responsible for AAP Implosion

This turmoil within the Aam Aadmi Party (AAP) is not around ideological and political issues. This struggle for power is just limited to the personal ambitions of a mot-ley group of 'do-gooder, anti-corruption reformists' who want to capture power within the party A section of party leaders say that inner-party democracy and transparency, which were the foundational guid-ing principles for internal decision-making, have been flouted and their efforts to restore them have set a model of behaviour.

The central issue that concerns the public of Delhi is not who is able to occupy the seat of authority to guide and control AAP. The Indian public, both in Delhi and outside, is keen to know the real ideological worldview of this party and its founding leaders on crucial national issues raised by the Sangh parivar. Does AAP consider the spread of the ideology of Hindu Rashtravad the main challenge to a plural, diverse, and secular India? Is there public evidence to suggest that the leadership of AAP firmly stands up to the challenge of the Hindu Rashtravadis?

A few facts may be mentioned to substantiate the argument that AAP has neither intellectually nor politico-ideologically taken up firm positions against the Rashtriya Swayamsevak Sangh (RSS) and the Narendra Modi-led central government. First, the anti-corruption movement of Anna Hazare brought together all strands of conflicting and contradictory ideologies in the same tabernacle. Personalities of the BJP and the RSS were visible on the public platform of Hazare. Second, the AAP leadership has repeatedly asserted in public that they do not believe in ideological positions of the Left or the Right and the implication of such a posturing is that the party's problems and policies are guided in a pragmatic manner. This party of 'pragmatists' was not at all shocked when Shazia Almi or Kiran Bedi walked over to the BJP because Hazare and the AAP leadership have shown that the Hindu rashtravadi BJP is not distinguishable from the non-ideological AAP leadership.

Third, it has been of no concern to AAP that the BJP's social base remains intact and Delhi politics, irrespective of the 2015 elections, remains solidly behind the Hindutwavadis. The secular vote shifted from the Congress to AAP because the Congress has not been perceived to be a winning party.

Should there be a split in AAP, it will not have any great consequence for society at large.

The Hindustan Times, 11 March, 2015

4

Two Agendas: One Modi

Prime Minister Narendra Modi during his one year of undisputed and unchallenged leadership of the Indian State had to single-handedly carry on his shoulders an extremely contradictory complex agenda of rising to the expectations of the Hindu Sangh Parivar on one hand and on the other the capitalist class. The public celebrations have been focused on the so-called achievements of the one year of the Narendra Modi government with a view to communicate with the various sections of the public about government's achievements. However the one-year celebrations are focused on peripheral basis. Because the real evaluation of Narendra Modi has to be undertaken by analysing the role of his government in promoting the agenda of Hindu Sangh Parivar led by the RSS and also taking steps to satisfy the real interests of the big industrial and business classes of India. The rationale for such an exercise is based on the fact that Modi is nothing without the RSS and its support and also, his track record of chief ministership of Gujarat state government from 2001 to 2014 provides clear evidence that Modi is a great champion of monopoly capitalist class of India. Modi has been shouting from the housetop about his "Model of Gujarat

Development" which in reality meant promotion of capitalism in Gujarat by development showcasing Gujarat government's constructive and positive approach to Indian and foreign investors for development.

Is Modi capable of resolving conflicts and contradictions, if any, between his two agendas of political Hinduism and enthusiastic and active championship of Indian and foreign monopoly capitalism? Modi was admonished by Barack Obama on January 29, 2014 for 'not protecting the life and property of minorities in his country'. Modi as a great champion of foreign investors from advanced western industrial capitalist countries cannot ignore such a warning by Obama because public opinion in the USA and European Union and Human Rights' watchdog groups will turn against Modi government if legitimate rights of minorities are violated in India. Modi cannot forget the post-Godhra anti-Muslim riots in February-April, 2002. The Gujarat chief minister was not welcomed by any western country and his foreign travel plans from 2002 to 2014 were jeopardised because Human Rights' groups in western capitalist countries had successfully blocked his visits because of his government's failure to protect the life and property of the minority Muslims in Ahmedabad in February-April, 2002. How can Modi ignore this harsh reality of international censorship when minority communities feel persecuted under his government at the centre?

Communal Agenda

The track record of Modi government at the centre from May 26, 2014 to May 2015, is not at all clean because Churches have been vandalised in the capital city of New

Delhi in 2014-2015. Members of the parliament belonging to the BJP have openly undertaken anti-Muslim activities like; reconversion of Muslims to Hinduism, actively encouraging Hindu-Muslim conflict leading to violence against Muslims, engineering anti-Muslim disputes over the location of some of the local mosques, the line of hurting Hindu sentiments by Muslims for their attitudes towards the cow, considered holy by the Hindu Sangh Parivar etc. Modi has adopted a two-fold approach while dealing with these core issues which are quite near and dear to the Hindu RSS and all its affiliates. If, on one hand, Modi has refused to take any cognizance or notice of anti-Muslim and anti-Christian actions of the Hindu RSS and its affiliates, on the other hand, he has only asked his Hindu joint family fraternity not to make reckless anti-minority statements in public ostensibly with a view that public image of his government is not tainted in western industrial capitalist countries. Modi has not spoken a single word about the riots in Atali (Ballabgarh) in Haryana which happened on May 25-26, 2015 and he has not taken any notice of frightened Muslims of Atali taking refuge in police stations for the safety against Hindu jat rioters. Modi has not visited the riot victims of Atali. However, on June, 2015, Modi made a public statement that, "Some unfortunate comments have been made, which were totally uncalled for. Our constitution guarantees religious freedom to every citizen and that is not negotiable. I have said it before and I say it again, any discrimination or violence against any community will not be tolerated." Modi has said it for public consumption, especially for western countries and their governments. Is Modi oblivious of the violence against Muslims in Atali or Muzaffarnagar? Modi is feeding and patronising the agenda of Hindu Rashtravaad and there is a firm government of Modi to promote political Hinduism under his authority as head of central government of India.

Promoting Globalisation

Modi has not forgotten his second agenda of giving a push forward in integrating Indian monopoly capitalism with global finance-capital led by the triad of imperialist countries like the United States of America, European Union and Japan. This aggressive pursuit of strengthening the joint alliance of domestic capitalism and the capitalism of imperialist countries has definitely the aim for both the partners to accumulate profit. The ongoing process of complete integration of the Indian State and the capitalist classes especially beginning with 1991 has brought the leaders of Indian monopoly classes directly into the corridors of the Indian State power and incidentally individual fortunes of monopolists have seen some shifts because of individual preferences of the chief political executive and Narendra Modi's preference is for Gujarati capitalists, especially Adani. If Bloomberg Billionaire's Index May 2014-2015 is a guide, in one year of Modi's government, the net worth stands thus: Gautam Adani 8.1 billion dollars, Dilip Shangvi 20.1 billion dollars, Shiv Nadar 14.1 billion dollars, L.N. Mittal 14.4 billion dollars, Azim Premji 15.1 billion dollars, Pallonji Mistry 15.5 billion dollars, and Mukesh Ambani 27.3 billion dollars. The change in the net worth of these billionaires in this one year is highest – +48.8 percent for Adani and negative, –32 percent of Mukesh Ambani. The State behaves as a minimal player before the power and influence of these billionaires and powerful transnational of imperialist United States of America, European Union and Japan. If the Modi government is bending before monopolists and political Hinduism of the Hindu Sangh Parivar, it is not at all bothered about unemployment in the country and also deepening of inequality and depreciation of the majority of underclass and lower middle class. The one year of Modi government has plagued India on religious communal lines and also it has accentuated and deepened social and economic cleavages on class, caste and region basis. This is one year of Modi in India which he is "celebrating".

People's Democracy, 9-10 June, 2015

5
Politics RSS Plays

Prime Minister Narendra Modi, under pressure at home and from abroad, felt compelled to state that "my government will not allow any religious group, belonging to the majority or the minority, to incite hatred against others, overtly or covertly". Addressing Christians in Delhi on February 17, Modi said, "My government will ensure that there is complete freedom of faith and that everyone has the undeterred right to retain or adopt the religion of his or her choice without coercion or under interference."

It is necessary to state clearly that neither Modi, an RSS pracharak himself, believes in the ideology of religious freedom for all nor his words and statements on this fundamental issue of India's secularism carry any weight with his parent organisation – Rashtriya Swayamsevak Sangh (RSS). It becomes clear from the statement of Mohan Bhagwat, the RSS chief who, while addressing a meeting of top RSS workers and members of its 40, affiliate bodies on February 17, stated about Modi that "he has will power, we should trust our swayamsevak". Obviously to implement the Sangh ideology as Prime Minister, it is crystal clear that in the Sangh Parivar the final centre of power is the RSS boss and the real power flows from the Nagpur headquarters of the RSS chief and his working committee.

Bhagwat has not left any one in doubt that he is in real command over the actions and ideological pronouncements of all swayamsevaks including Prime Minister Modi. This is the reason that the focus should be on the RSS chief and his public pronouncements as well as his actions. It has become essential because the RSS had always claimed, especially whenever it was challenged, that it was a "cultural" and not a political organisation. RSS had always worn this mask of political neutrality to carry on its agenda of 'Hinduisation' of India.

It has become imperative to completely expose the reality of the role of RSS in public life. As Bhagwat, unlike his predecessors in the RSS, does not feel any compulsion while speaking in public about RSS's real goals in politics. Every statement and action of Bhagwat is meant to clearly convey to the Modi government at the Centre and all BJP-led state governments that they should blindly implement and do not mess up with the "agenda" of the RSS and its 40 organisations and affiliates.

A few public statements of Bhagwat deserve to be mentioned here to demonstrate that this cultural czar has been openly and unambiguously setting the "agenda" of the BJP-led governments. While addressing the academic council meeting of Punjabrao Vidyapeeth in Nagpur, he observed that the "time is ripe... and we all must grab this opportunity to bring about a desired change at the earliest..." He further elaborated, "In the past 1,200 years one mindset has been polluted and influenced by the val-ues of people and forces that attacked Bharat and ruled over here. We need to wipe out this influence completely by decolonising our minds with sustained and constant efforts." This statement of Bhagwat was carried in RSS mouthpiece *Organiser* on December 2014 so that every swayamsevak should start moving and implement the agenda of "correcting the past" which was handed over by Muslim invaders. Following this hideous advice, External Affairs Minister Sushma Swaraj quickly demanded that teaching of *Bhagwat Gita,* the sacred Hindu scripture, be made a compulsory reading in all schools of India.

The RSS chief made every effort to ensure that the agenda of Hindutva was implemented by the government of the day as he had single-handedly worked hard beginning in 2013 to project Modi as the BJP chief election campaigner and later on its prime ministerial nominee. All this has been the handiwork of Bhagwat, who had actively worked for the victory of BJP in the Lok Sabha elections. Secondly, Bhagwat has focussed his attention upon expansion and establishment of RSS workshops, known as shakhas, where RSS recruits are trained and equipped to learn the ideology of Hindutva and Hindu Rashtravaad. It has also been stated that Bhagwat has been able to increase the number of RSS shakhas. K.B. Hedgewar, the founder of RSS in 1925, had defined the agenda of shakhas as training of Hindu youths in martial arts to face Muslim enemies. He blended teaching of ideology with quasi-military like training to enable the youths to protect and defend Hindus who were being threatened by Muslims. Bhagwat has made arrangements for the recruitment to RSS through website and other methods of modern communication. It would have been difficult for RSS founder Hedgewar to ensure the speed of expansion of RSS shakhas and the number of cadres and new recruits as it is happening in 2015 under the stewardship of Bhagwat.

Thirdly, the RSS, beginning with 1925 till 2015, has indoctrinated its new recruits and cadres on the basis of an ideology in which Hindus have been projected as "victims" and hence they have to 'defend' themselves. Bhagwat, while addressing a three-day annual meeting of over 390 office-bearers of various offshoots of the Sangh Parivar including BJP in Lucknow on October 19, 2014, thought it fit to issue a warning that "an individual leader, a slogan, a party, a government and miracles alone cannot bring about positive change in society and nation." Continuing further, he exhorted "conspiracies were being hatched against Hindu society and that such conspiracies should be exposed". Conspiracies against Hindus and defence of Hindus have been a running theme of the RSS ideologues and Bhagwat has reiterated it again and again. Is it surprising that "*Ghar Wapsi*" (conversion or re-conversion) events have emerged on the scene during the nine months of the Modi government? Is it surprising that "love Jihad" has become a campaign issue of hatred against Muslims by the RSS? Is it unexpected that six churches have been vandalised or burnt in less than two months of 2015 in the capital city of Delhi? Politics of targeting of the minorities is an integral part of the ideology of Hindutva, and Bhagwat is openly preaching and practicing this ideology, which is fundamental to its organisational network.

Fourth and finally, organisational and ideological structures of RSS need a little reference as the source of authoritarian control exercised by Bhagwat is because he is the unchallenged boss of RSS. The RSS is hierarchically organised along with an iron chain of command over all swayamsevaks and every disciplined swayamsevak is controlled by a higher and superior functionary and this chain of authority finally ends with the sarsanghchalak as envisaged by K.B. Hedgewar. At present, sarsanghchalak Bhagwat is the undisputed commander-in-chief whose commands, or words or statements are like a code of conduct for every RSS worker, irrespective of his or her areas of operations in any of the 40 RSS organisations including BJP. Further, beginning with V.D. Savarkar and founder Hedgewar, the ideology to be followed by every swayamsevak, irrespective of his assignment, as defined by RSS is what Bhagwat reiterated on January 4, 2015 that "India was a Hindu nation". Repeating it on February 9, he stated, "We need to ensure one language, one god and one religion." This ideologically well defined doctrine is a belief system of every RSS worker and it is left to Rajnath Singh, the Home Minister of India, to set the record straight when he observed on November 22,2014 that "RSS is not an external force. I am from the RSS, the Prime Minister himself is a RSS volunteer. We (RSS members) are from childhood and will remain till we are alive." "When we ourselves are from the RSS then what interference will it have to wield (on the government)?" he exclaimed.

If this is the crux of the issue, the statement of Modi on February 17 assuring that the government will respect religious freedom is phoney and spurious because it is for Bhagwat to exercise full control over the actions of the BJP governments and the Prime Minister or BJP Chief Ministers do not enjoy any ideological and political autonomy and this led the Supreme Court on February 9, 2015 to observe that "India till now is a secular country. We do not know for how long it will remain a secular country. We have to stamp put religion from civil laws. It is very necessary. There are already too many problems." If the Supreme Court is concerned about the prospects of the survival of secular state of India, it deserves to be taken note of because the Supreme Court has always maintained that "secularism constitutes the basic structure of the Constitution". The upshot of the above narrative is that organizations controlled by the Mohan Bhagwat-led RSS are actively operating against religious minorities and it is Bhagwat not Prime Minister Modi who is at the helm of affairs. Hence, Bhagwat in politics is pursuing ruthlessly the agenda of Hinduisation of Indian society and the Modi government is working under his commands because he is the real repository of authority in the RSS.

—*People's Democracy, March 9-15, 2015*

6

Modi—The End Game of Autonomy

The BJP-Sangh parivar led Narendra Modi government at the centre during its eight months of rule has single handedly accelerated, even completely cemented, the integration of Indian monopoly capitalism with the imperialist centres of finance-capital of the developed industrialised countries. The process of integration of India with global finance-capital needs to be properly contextualised to substantiate the argument that Modi has taken the process to its logical end by enthusiastically pursuing public policies during the eight months of his rule which has clearly brought India under the complete shadow of global finance-capital and transnational capitalism of the developed centres of global capitalism. The process of opening of the Indian national market to foreign capital investors had begun in 1990 under the leadership of prime minister P.V. Narasimha Rao and finance minister Manmohan Singh. The Rao-Manmohan model of free market economy commonly described as the system of liberalisation, globalisation and privatisation was a complete rupture with the post-independence model of State-led planned development on the basis of self-reliance, import substitution system of industrialisation. The model of self-reliance economic development was followed by the ruling groups of the Indian State by safeguarding country's relative autonomy. India never followed the policy of isolation while dealing with the international post-Second World War centres of power, on the contrary, India actively participated and interacted with the bipolar global bloc system on the basis of policies of non-alignment without becoming a camp follower of any of the global power bloc. The policy of non-alignment followed by India during post-independence period was promised on the belief that a sovereign state should take its own decisions by keeping in mind material interests as defined by its citizens. The policy of self-reliant economic development and foreign policy of non-alignment in power bloc politics were two sides of the same coin which protected national goal of autonomy of Indian State. Foreign aid was welcomed without political strings because it was considered a necessary 'evil' for development of a backward developing economy of an erstwhile colony and terms and conditions for receiving foreign aid for investments were negotiated by Indians with the aid-givers on the basis Of equality, modality and priorities to be defined by the Indian Planning Commission.

This model of economics and politics which ensured autonomy of Indian public policy matters was completely abandoned in 1990 and it was replaced by the mode of free market economy and invitation to foreign transnational corporations and international funding institutions like the World Bank, the IMF, private investors and government funds for investment from capital surplus centres of capitalism. It is not only the old model of economic planning of market economy which was abandoned by Narasimha Rao-Manmohan Singh in 1990, the policy of non-alignment was also given farewell when the Rao government recognised the theocratic state of Israel essentially because Western centres of capitalism led by America wanted India to legitimise the Israeli Jewish state leaving behind the traditional friendship with Palestine which have been always a victim of Israeli aggression supported by America. It is not an accident that in 2015, beginning with 1990, India has integrated itself with Israeli defence production industry and has been lukewarm towards the Palestinians. It deserves to be mentioned here with great emphasis that during the eight months of prime ministership, Modi has travelled to every country except Arab countries from where oil supplies and remissions of Indians are eagerly awaited. It is Israel and not the Arab world which is the top priority of Modi and a fact which illustrates that the Indian State's chief political executive is determined to make India, a zone of influence of western capitalism. President Barack Obama-Narendra Modi parleys in Delhi from January 25 to 27,2015 have to be seen in this context with a rider that Modi himself is ideologically and politically committed to become a willing party for bringing India under the umbrella of global finance-capital. Three important documents issued at the meetings of Obama and Modi on January 26, provide a framework for substantiating the central argument that Modi government has willingly and voluntarily bid goodbye to 'relative autonomy of the State' of India.

The three documents are the Joint Statement, the US-India Joint Strategic union for the Asia-Pacific and Indian Ocean region and the Indo-US Declaration of Friendship. A clinical analysis of the main implications and meanings of these documents should begin with a statement that the Modi government has not only integrated Indian 'economy' with global capitalism, it has gone a Step forward, for the first time, to integrate India's 'defence system' with the Western industrialised capitalist countries by 'opening' defence production sector to private investors with Indian and foreign origin. The Manmohan Singh government vacillated on defence sector investment ceiling; the Modi government did not hesitate for a moment to raise the ceiling from 27 per cent to 49 per cent for private investors. It is for the opposition parties to expose the Modi government on any underhand understanding given to Obama on Nuclear Liability Act and other pernicious tie ups made by Modi with Obama. A great concern for Indians should be around serious implications of 'Joint Strategic union for Asia-Pacific and Indian Ocean region' because America has announced that it is 'Rebalancing' its Asia policy and Asia-Pacific is the "pivot" of future strategic alliances especially among the countries including the United States, Japan, Australia and also to involve India in this alliance. Obama observed on January 26, that 'US can be India's best partner'. China promptly reacted strongly on this Joint Statement on South China Sea disputes and urged that the 'third parties do not get involved'. China went further on January 26 and bluntly warned India that Washington wants to put "neighbours against neighbours" and gave an advice to India not to fall in this 'trap' laid down by America.

Is Modi changing the objectives and context of foreign strategic policy by firmly allying with Asia-Pacific game plans of America along with Japan and Australia and is Modi trying to build this 'alliance' against an Asian country like China? It deserves to be clearly stated that the Sangh Parivar and its loyal product Narendra Modi have always considered 'Muslim Pakistan' and Communist China as opponents of

India. Does Modi understand the changing dynamics of the second decade of twenty first century Asia and global strategic system? Why did China react strongly on January 26 against Obama-Modi Joint statement on Asia-Pacific and Indian Ocean region? Why army chief of Pakistan, Raheed Sharif did make a hurried visit to China for two days at the time when Obama was in Delhi? It is very easy to abandon the time tested foreign policy of non-alignment of India; it is dangerous to shift foreign strategic goals by allying with America and annoying neighbours like China and Pakistan. Does Modi understand that for the first time in post-Cold War phase of international relations, China and Russia are in the process of becoming strong allies and one of the goals of this powerful 'alliance' is to checkmate America in Asia? It is time that rights and freedom of maritime navigation in international water ways, seas and oceans should be guaranteed under International Law of Seas, however it does not mean that demand for freedom of navigation should lead to a collision course on South China Sea between India and China. The secular and democratic political parties have to be alert to the fact that Modi has not only abandoned foreign policy of non-alignment or abolished the Planning Commission by replacing it by Niti Aayog, he is pushing India towards a dangerous direction not only by integrating national economy with global finance-capital, he is determined to integrate India with imperialism by following foreign policy which is anti-China, anti-Pakistan and subservient to the United States of America.

Peoples Democracy, February 22, 2015

7

Ideological Politics of BJP in Power

The real essential goal of Hindu Sangh Parivar led and controlled by Mohan Bhagwat, the Rashtriya Swayamsevak Sangh is to control the State power and its apparatus and instruments to establish a Hindu State and society in India.

This is the reason why Mohan Bhagwat publically stated that it is for the first time after 67 years of India in Independence that a real Hindu government has been formed at the centre with RSS Pracharak Narendra Modi at the helm of affairs. The Sangh Parivar and its political shop, the BJP, clearly understand the meaning of State power in their hands, because it is for the first time that that the BJP has formed its own government on the basis of its own majority of 282 out of 543 Lok Sabha seats. They are using this extraordinary opportunity for spreading and strengthening its ideology of Hindutva. The Narendra Modi led government from May 26, 2014 to January 26, 2015, the Republic Day has taken many steps to achieve its goal of exercising governmental power at the centre to rewrite and reverse the philosophical agenda of the secular, democratic, pluralistic and welfarist contribution of the Indian republic. A few facts may be mentioned to substantiate the argument that all affiliates of the RSS controlled groups under the protective and pro-active umbrella of the Modi government have been working overtime to implement its anti-religious minority agenda for the last seven months. First, a clear method behind the madness of RSS groups and Hindu leaders is to tell Muslims and Christians that they are in wrong religious company because as "original Hindus" they should come back to Hindu religion and this *"ghar wapasi"* campaign has been publically launched because the Hindu government of Narendra Modi is not at all a stumbling block in this venture. The authenticity of "conversion" "reconversion" *"ghar wapasi"* campaigns of the RSS affiliates can be attributed to RSS supremo Mohan Bhagwat whose statements are like a command for all swayamsevaks. The oracle Bhagwat put a seal of approval on the obnoxious campaign when on December 20, 2014 while addressing Vishwa Hindu Parishad at Kolkata, he observed "Those who drifted away will be brought back to their original faith. If someone steals your belongings, it should finally come back to you." Religions except Hinduism are based on people who have gone "astray' and hence *"ghar wapasi"* is very relevant. The real meaning of this anti-conversion campaign is that the Sangh Parivar aVid the BJP-in-government does not accept constitutionally guaranteed freedom of religion and is trying to turn upside down the secular philosophical foundations of republic of India.

The secular parties launched as agitation against "conversion" campaign because it is against constitution. Mohan Bhagwat and Venkaiah Naidu of the BJP proposed that the opposition parties should agree to a common anti-conversion law for the whole country. The secular opposition rejected this proposal because the real meaning of "campaign for re-conversion" is to make religious minorities feel culturally inferior and second-class-citizens in Hindu India. Second, closely linked with the goal of making everyone in India a Hindu, is the demand of BJP MP Sakshi Maharaj that "the Hindu women should have more children" obviously with the goal of making India highly populated by Hindus only.

On one hand, the RSS led affiliates and the BJP does not respect rights of women to take decisions about themselves. On the other, by launching a notorious hate campaign on so-called "love jihad", by propagating that Muslim boys were courting Hindu girls to marry them and elope, they reduce women to a status of subordination and complete subjugation. The equal rights of women as guaranteed by the democratic republican constitution are undermined by the Sangh Parivar which wants to control a woman's right to marry a person of her own choice. Incidentally, it is a real fact that from K.B. Hedgewar (1925) to Mohan Bhagwat (2015) all supremos of the RSS have been male, and preferably brahmacharis.

The Modi government and the Sangh Parivar during the last seven months have packed every educational and cultural organisation with RSS activists and other Sangh and BJP committed supporters. The Censor Board chief, Leela Samson resigned on January 16 and publicly alleged that the present government was "interfering" in the work of film certification. Arun Jaitley made an offensive statement on January 17 on her resignation and labelled her as a "UPA government appointee". As if this is not enough, the BJP government on January 19 appointed Pahlaj Nihalani as chairman of the Central Board of Film Certification along with actors owing allegiance to the BJP and the RSS and the cat was out of the bag when Nihalani on January 20, just a day after his appointment, declared that he was with the BJP and Narendra Modi. The story does not end here; the educational and cultural agenda for the Hinduisation of all institutions of society imparting education to children in schools, colleges and universities where Hindu scriptures like *Bhagwat Gita*, *Mahabharatha* and *Ramayana* versions as certified by priests of Sangh Parivar along with Sanskrit has to be taught. Smriti Irani, the HRD minister is following the Sangh Parivar Itihas Organisation's order to "correct" history textbooks and to see to it that they are "re-written" from Hindu perspective and this is the reason why the NCERT director Sinclair, like Samson of Censor Board, has been given marching orders by the government for making a place for a Hindu Rashtravadi historian as it has been done in the case of Indian Council for Historical Research. The Sangh Parivar and the BJP ministers like prime minister and home minister have been "glorifying" Ancient India for all wisdom including scientific knowledge of high order. The State power is exercised by the Modi government to inculcate values which are anti-modern: science and brahmanical Hindu symbols like surya namaskar and Hindu temples have gained great legitimacy under this government of "Bhagwa Dhwajya." Muslims are targeted for indulging in "cow slaughter" activities and such identification by the BJP governments creates a great sense of insecurity and anxiety among the Muslims. Finally, intolerance of democratic right of dissent has become a "norm" during the last seven months of the Narendra Modi government and all sorts of obscurantist communal casteist groups have felt encouraged to 'coerce" those with whom they differ. One another example is of Tamil writer Perumal Murugan, whose novel *Madhorubagan* translated into English as *One Part Woman* had to declare on Facebook on January 16-17 that "Perumal, the writer, is dead" because of protests against him launched by sectarian Hindu and casteist groups. The above facts have been mentioned to reiterate the larger ideological and political line that the real meaning of State power for the forces of Sangh Parivar is to homogenise India of great diversities and pluralities into one Hindu Rashtra.

It is not BJP-in-government at the centre and in states, it is the RSS led Sangh Parivar which is in the real driver's seat and is controlling all the institutional and ideological apparatus of the Indian State to achieve its ideological goal of establishing Hindu State in the mirage of so-called Ancient Hindu India. The State is always an important centre of power for the fanatically committed "ideologues" like the present rulers in India.

The plea here is that a focus on the Modi government's policies and programmes to hand over India to foreign and Indian monopoly and capitalist classes should be a critical issue, however the larger ideological project of State power in the hands of RSS should not be ignored at all. The ideological superstructure plays an important role in shaping and making of a society.

Peoples Democracy, February 8, 2015

8

Saffronization of Education

The RSS and all its affiliates including the BJP are committed to spread and strengthen its distinctive ideology of Hindutva by recruiting and training Hindu youth in its daily Shakhas, and if in government pursued and implement its ideologically driven educational framework from schools to colleges and universities. It is not without reason that Mohan Bhagawat, the current Supremo of the RSS addressed in Delhi on November 25, 2014 an eminent group of 250 educationist including Vice-Chancellors and UGC Chairman clearly observed that there is a need for a "Nationalist education" framework and the teaching of "Nationalist scriptures" in educational institutes. Ms Smriti Irani, the HRD Minister in Narendra Modi Government, was instructed on October 30, 2014 to "take suggestions and seek perspectives" from RSS affiliates like Akhil Bharatiya Vidyarthi Parishad, Vidhya Bharati, Vivekanand International Foundation and on October 30, 2014 the RSS asked Ms. Irani to "correct" the history taught in schools "to highlight Indian heroes, and the role played by Hindu culture and it in shaping the country." Ms. Irani on its Sixth meeting with the RSS on October 30, 2014 "the representatives told the minister that the future generation should learn the true history of India." A clear mandate of the RSS to BJP Governments is to mend and mould its educational policies, programs and institutions to spread the message of Hindu Sanatan Dharma culture and to assure this Mohan Bhagawat on February 18, 2015 observed that "He (Narendra Modi) has will power; we should trust our Swaymsevak." This is the reason that BJP Governments whether at the Centre or in the States are at work to achieve their primary ideological goal of Hinduisation of education through educational institutions like schools, colleges and universities. First, every functionary involved in the job of policy making or implementation of educational programme of any kind has to be "committed" to the educational ideology of Sangh Parivar. The National Council of Educational Research and Training, the most important institution engaged in educational activities of the schools throughout India was targeted by HRD and its Director Parvin Sinclair was forced to resign to make way for the appointee of the Government on ideological considerations. Second, Dinanath Batra, an RSS pracharak and one time president of Shiksha Sanskriti Uttam Nyas has been appointed head of Educational Commission of Haryana by the BJP state Government and his non-scientific and ideological books on 'character building and value education of Hindu culture' have been prescribed by BJP government of Gujarat schools. Third, if on one hand all public educational institutions have to be managed by RSS-BJP affiliated individuals from Vice-chancellors to school teachers, on the other the RSS has been active in establishing its own educational institutions like Shishu Niketans, Bal Bharatis, Vidya Bhawans and its special focus is to Hinduise through educating the tribal population or Vanvasis of India.

The story does not end here. It is not only that BJP governments are appointing its own ideologically committed members of the Parivar in all educational institutions, its attempts to Hinduise Indian culture through education are much beyond the role of formal education which is under its control. The crux of the time is the philosophical and ideological basic framework of the Hindu Sangh parivar on the basis of which it wants to mould and hegemonise the whole society and impact its belief systems, thinking and cultural ways of life and beliefs. The Bharatiya Shiksha Mandal (BSM 1969) observed on October 25, 2014 that its goal is "to imbue bharatiya education with bharatiyata" and undertake radical 'corrective to history text books' to purge them of all foreign influences and achieve the goal defined by V.D. Savarkar to 'Hinduise the nation' arid Mohan Bhagawat following in the footsteps of its founders beginning with K.B. Hedgewar (1925) on February 9, 2015 "We need to ensure one language, one God and one religion" and philosophical education of Indians is contained in 'national scriptures' *Bhagwat Gita* which has answers to everybody's problems. It is not a mere rhetoric the BJP state Government of Haryana has made compulsory teaching of Bhagawat Gita in schools for primary and secondary levels. All ancient texts like Vedas, Bhagawat Gita and other Sanskrit language text as interpreted by Brahmins who knew Sanskrit language contains every truth which needs to be taught and message which has to be spread. The claim is that Hindu India and its Munis and Rishis and their spoken and written words have to be communicated to every generation of Hindus to take pride in their past glories and heights to which Hindu India had reached.

The only Great Cultural Traditions which has to be the guide of Hindu nation building is contained in the wisdom inherited by the Hindu natives of India as Bhagawat said on November 26, 2014 that the indigenous education system based on ancient Indian values and knowledge base has to be revived because we already have storehouse of knowledge. The RSS and BJP Governments following the above logic are targeting the culture and educational institutions of 'foreigners' or 'outsiders' like Muslims and Christians, mosques and Churches, Madrassa, missionary schools to cleanse Hindu education from the polluted influences of non Hindu like other religious minority groups. The VHP targeted the Christian Missionary Schools in Bastar District, a region of Chattisgargh and asked the Catholic Schools to have goddess Saraswati idol installed in their schools and on Nov 21-22, 2014 seven Church representatives and 12 VHP members met to ask Headmaster of these schools that students be asked to address schools principals instead of Father as "pracharya" or "up-pracharya" or "Sir" and every schools in BJP states has to begin its day with Hindu prayers like Surya Namaskar, recitation of Gayatri Mantra and worship of Goddess Saraswati. The only subject matter to be taught is derived from Great Hindu Tradition to create a strong Hindu Rashtra, what V.D. Savarkar asked "militarize the Hindus" or K.B. Hedgewar stabilized RSS Shakhas to make Hindus physically strong who can fight against 'foreigners' within India like Muslims and Christians.

The upshot of above narrative is education for Hinduisation of whole society is the primary and pre-eminent agenda of RSS led BJP Governments of Narendra Modi or earlier Atal Bihari Vajpayee (1998-2004) and every

Chief Minister and this specific and special agenda is monitored very closely by the RSS Supremo and his colleagues who act as watchdog of BJP-in-governments. Every other action or decision of every educational functionary under BJP governments is integrally linked with this grand goal only.

9

Cooperative Federalism: Reality or Myth?

A Public policy statement made by Prime Minister Narendra Modi deserves a clinical analysis and a close scrutiny because the real meaning behind publicly stated goals may be lying hidden and it is essential to bring into public focus the reality of pronouncements and announcements of the prime minister. Modi has claimed that his government is determined to usher in the era of 'Cooperative federalism' and 'Competitive federalism' in place of the earlier systems of centralised federalism in which the state governments were reduced to the states of subordinates to the central government's overwhelming authority over all the 29 states and 7 union territories of India. The first step taken by the Modi government to make people believe the new federal balance of power is being created has been the abolition of sixty-five year old institution of Planning Commission of India which has been replaced by a 'think tank' like the National Institution for Transforming India, popularly described as the NITI Ayog. The centralised federal system of sixty-five years of post-independence India is a child of the system of centralised planning and if a new system of federal relations has to be stabilised, the old centralising institution has to be abolished and replaced by a new one like the NITI Ayog. Modi addressed a meeting of all chief ministers of the states and union territories to announce this grand new design of federalism by making a statement that a chief minister, unlike the past, will not have to look towards the centre for policy guidance and fiscal resources because in the new scheme of 'fiscal federalism', the share of resources of each state will be transferred to be spent by the state government in an 'autonomous' manner depending on their own priorities which will be decided by each and every state on its own.

The Modi government in pursuit of its commitment for 'New Federalism' tabled in parliament on February 24, 2015 the recommendation of the Fourteenth Finance Commission of India. The salient feature of new fiscal federalism is that there is a ten per cent increase in the share of states in the centre's tax revenue from earlier 32 per cent to 42 per cent The government stated that the states will have freedom to plan their own expenditure priorities and Modi himself stated that the "states are free to change" centrally sponsored schemes and they should "decide for themselves". Modi's hyperbolic language stated that the new Team India will be of all chief ministers who will be 'partners' in the governing council of NITI Ayog. Arun Jaitley, the finance minister, said that all "Centrally sponsored schemes are discretionary. Payments should end," and in spite of Abhijeet Sen's note of dissent appended to the Fourteenth Finance Commission, the Modi government has steamrolled its new project of 'Cooperative federalism' without paying any attention to the different needs of different states like 'deficit states or the backward regions' or the states under debt The states of Bengal, Bihar, Orissa, Assam have all protested against such a steamroller approach because of their special situations in which the central government has to provide special funds to these states.

The Modi government's rhetoric of new 'fiscal federalism' and 'cooperative federation' in which the state governments are freed from the excessive controls of the central government is oblivious of the reality of diversities of India in which developed states co-exist with relatively less developed and extremely backward states and one formula of fiscal distribution cannot meet the requirements of all different 'categories' of the states and union territories. It is not only that the Modi government has completely ignored the complex and contradictory situations which prevail 'across the states', its tall claims of deconcentration and decentralisation of powers of the central government while dealing with the state governments is quite untenable in the light of a few salient facts mentioned here to substantiate the argument that behind the facade of cooperative federalism lies the real goal of centralisation of Modi's authority over the whole of India. First, Modi is enthusiastically pursing political economy of liberalisation, globalisation and privatisation (LGP) and completely opening the Indian market to both Indian and foreign monopoly capitalist classes and in this grand project Modi's asking all the states to follow the 'one model of political economy' as laid down by the central government and open its markets to private capital, both Indian and foreign. Modi's politics of economies is to facilitate the establishment of capitalist economic system for the 'whole country' in which all chief ministers will be in his language the 'Team India'. The Modi government's real game then is to make all chief ministers fall in line and follow the path of development as decided by the oligarchic class of India and abroad so that capitalism takes deep roots in Indian society. It is not without reason that the Modi government is going out of the way to persuade and bribe all the chief ministers to accept Goods and Services Tax system for the whole country and make India one national market of capitalist system. Is it diversity or uniformity in the garb of cooperative and competitive federalism? Second, the Modi government has appointed all governors for the states who belong to the Rashtriya Swayamsevak Sangh to keep firm control over chief ministers especially non-BJP state governments like that of Uttar Pradesh, Bihar or Karnataka. All these RSS loyalist governors are eyes and ears of the central government to keep surveillance over the state governments so that they do not deviate from the path shown by the centre. Third, the real Hindu Rashtravadi, Modi and the real controller of the Modi-led government Mohan Bhagwat, believe in establishing ideological hegemony over the whole of India and in this hegemonic project there is no space for dissent, difference or devolution of ideas and power. M.S. Golwakar, the real consolidated of RSS, had clearly stated that India was 'attacked' by foreigners because it was a 'divided country' and hence he pleaded for a highly "centralised system of government to maintain unity of Hindu India and the creation of 50 administrative units for the governance of the whole of Bharat Mata". How can state governments be autonomous in any manner under a regime of centralised ideology of Hindutva for the whole country? It is not only that Modi himself believes and practices the system of centralised governance and concentration of power in his own hands; he is also a faithful messenger of centralised hegemonic ideology of Hindutva. It is a deadly combination where a prime minister primarily believes in controlling all the levers of power in his own hands and his prime minister's office and he also practices centralised Hindutva ideology which he has learnt in the workshop or school of Rashtriya Swayamsevak Sangh.

Hence Modi's cooperative federalism is another name for centralisation and control over the whole country. Fiscal federalism is only pretence to facilitate the emergence of capitalist market system for the whole country, without any exception, and the real face of Modi is reflected in the mirror as of a full-fledged and full blooded centraliser who cannot deviate from the ideology of Hindutva. Modi's preference for a decentralised federalism is a myth because the reality is that he is guiding the whole county in one direction of capitalism and Hindu Rashtra. This is the political economy of Modi's federalism project, otherwise there is no explanation for the ruthless aggressive policy of the RSS to expand in eastern India especially the North East. If Modi believes in federal diversity, he should not be presiding over the expansion of the forces of Hindutva in the tribal belt of the North East. This is the crux of the issue.

Peoples Democracy, 5 April, 2015

10

Modi on Minority Issues

It is for the first time in the history of post-Independent India that, the prime minister has been compelled to defend himself publicly that he is fully committed to the constitutional values of secularism. This affirmation by media, unfortunately for the whole country, has been made in American magazine Time, to which he gave an interview published on May 7 to 8, 2015. What is the reason for a prime minister of a sovereign democratic republic to defend his domestic policy before a foreign audience?

A few facts may be mentioned to contextualise the real significance of Narendra Modi's interview to the *Time* magazine. First, pro-imperialist Modi not only proclaimed America as "natural ally" of India, but he has also taken great credit for arranging Barack Obama's visit on the Republic Day this year. However, this achievement of Modi was short lived because Obama just before his return asked Modi to provide full security and protection to religious minorities like Christians and Muslims. Modi was really stung because of such a public statement by the US president. Second, the annual report of the United States Committee on International Religious Freedom of 2015 castigated the Modi government on minority policies like '*Ghar Wapsi*' or on

Christian Missionaries, and observed that "Muslim communities are facing undue security and arbitrary arrests and detentions." Third, if the tenure of Modi's conduct as prime minister for one year is only seen in the larger context that Modi as chief minister of Gujarat from post-Godhra riots of 2002 to May 26, 2014 had been declared a 'persona non-grata' by the United States and European Union countries and was denied "visa" to visit these countries for his alleged role in post-Godhra anti-Muslim riots in which about 2,000 innocents were killed and about 3,00,000 Muslims had to seek protection in the "refugee camps" in Ahmedabad.

Modi, personally as chief minister, was an "unwanted" individual and his entry to the US and Europe was banned. Fourth, in this age of information explosion, Modi as chief minister of Gujarat from 2001 to 2014, had created a situation where every Muslim was a suspect in spite of the fact that his own minister was punished by the court for actively promoting inter-religious hostility and leading to riots against Muslims, and terrorist attack against Akshardham temple in Ahmedabad was immediately linked to Muslims and the arrested Muslims were all acquitted after 12 years of imprisonment because the court found them "innocent". It was publicly claimed by all governments that "terrorists" have no religion, the fact of the matter is every terrorist attacks including the one on Samjhauta Express train from Delhi to Pakistan has been attributed to Muslims while fanatic Hindus trained by extremist Hindu organisations have been found "guilty" of indulging in terrorist activities. The banned Student Islamic Movement of India is suspected and its associates are arrested as a matter of routine after every serious violent incident. The spread of the ideology of Hindutva in the country has led to a situation where the Hindu opportunists and police force point their fingers against Muslims as culprits. This is the domestic content well known to the international community and it led Modi to observe in his interview to American *Time* magazine that "my government will not tolerate or accept any discrimination based on caste, creed and religion. So there is no place for imaginary apprehensions with regard to the rights of minorities in India". This public statement of Modi that, "apprehensions are imaginary" deserve to be completely exposed so that he cannot get away with his false claims to "defend the secular Constitution of India".

What is the real story of religious minorities in India under the ongoing Hinduisation of society, polity and culture? It deserves to be clearly emphasised here that the determined manner in which BJP governments at the Centre and in some states are pursuing the Hindu ideological agenda has created a sense of fear, insecurity and anxiety among religious minorities like Muslims and Christians who are feeling threatened by the actions and policy statements of the BJP as all public policies are loaded against religious and cultural identities and beliefs of the minorities. The BJP and the affiliates of RSS have developed a feeling that they occupy the centre state of Indian society, polity and culture and this self-confidence has been revealed by public assertion of RSS supreme Mohan Bhagwat on March 14, 2015 while addressing Akhil Bharatiya Pratinidhi Sabha that "we are all Hindus...all those born in India are Hindus. Whether they accept it or not they are culturally, nationally and DNA-wise the same". Elaborating the statement of RSS chief at the same meeting, RSS joint general secretary Dattatreya Hosabale observed, "Who do you call minorities? We don't consider anybody to be a minority. There should be no minority because in the country there is no minority." BJP and RSS with all its affiliates are working with patronage of governments led by Narendra Modi at the Centre and all the chief ministers of major states to push forward the agenda of Hindutva, defined by V.D. Savarkar. Ram Madhav, BJP general secretary, referred to the role played by RSS in the Lok Sabha elections of 2014 and said on April 12 that "the RSS chief categorically told our cadre that we are working because of historic reason that India needed a major political transformation", and this goal was achieved when BJP for the first time formed its own government at the Centre on May 26, 2014 on the basis of its own majority of 282 out of 543 members of the Lok Sabha. A few silent facts may be mentioned here to substantiate the argument that every government of the BJP under the supervision of the RSS chief pursued its ideological agenda which has sent a clear message to all major religious minorities that you are a "second-class-citizen" in Hindu India. First, it is targeting Muslim and Christian communities and their cultural and educational institutions by launching a movement by the Sangh Parivar for "re-conversion" or "*Ghar Wapasi*" of the minority groups to Hinduism. The issue of "religious conversion", a very sensitive issue, became an agenda of public discourse when Union ministers Rajnath Singh and Venkaiah Naidu and other tall leaders of BJP asked not only for a public debate but also wished to create national consensus for the need for a law against "conversion". Why has the BJP in government suddenly felt the need for a national debate in 2014-15 and the need for a national law of "religious conversions"? The answer is given by Mohan Bhagwat "make India a Hindu Rasthra". Will religious minorities feel secure at the height of this campaign by governments owing loyalty to one majority religion only?

Second, BJP governments and affiliates of the Hindu Sangh Parivar have once again made anti-cow slaughter law, a public issue because of the propaganda that holy cow of Hindus is eaten by Muslims who are non-Hindu. It is not surprising that only Muslims have been arrested for violating anti-cow slaughter laws by the state governments of the BJP. Third, if Yogi Adityanath of the BJP, as MP, has been openly indulging in hate campaigns against Muslim community, another MP Sakshi Maharaj on April 14, 2015 demanded that Muslims compulsorily undergo "vasectomy" to control galloping Muslim population and enforce "two-child norm" for Muslims. Fourth, while every religious community violence, known as Hindu-Muslim riot, has made minorities feel insecure, it is for the first time that the BJP nominated candidates for 2014 Lok Sabha who were "accused of instigating anti-Muslim riots in Muzaffarnagar in Uttar Pradesh".

The message is direct and unambiguous that Hindus indulging in violence against Muslims will be rewarded by the BJP or as in the case of massacre of Hashimpura, where 42-45 Muslims were massacred by UPPAC personnel on May 22, 1987, the minorities will have to wait for justice as in the judgment delivered on March 21, 2015 the judge observed with anguish that the "lives of innocent men have been taken by the state agency" and the 19 accused UPPAC personnel had to be "acquitted" because "one cannot be convicted on the basis of flimsy investigation which has gaps and holes". Can minorities have faith in the majesty of the rule of law when the state agencies are themselves communalised and the home minister of India did not utter a single word on such massacre of Muslims at the hands of "state agency". The government yet has not filed an appeal against acquittal.

The telling example of this "helplessness" by religious minorities has been provided specifically by Gujarat when after the communal riots of Ahmedabad and other areas from February 28 to April 2002 where the victim Muslim community sought protection by living in Muslim localities only. The growing "ghettoisation" of Muslims who prefer to live only in Muslim localities of their own is creating a wall of separation and suspicion between majority Hindus and minority Muslims. The explanation for this development is that Muslims do not feel protected by the state functionaries while in distress and they find collective security by living only in Muslim brotherhood.

It is not without reason that when prime minister or state home ministers condemn actions and statements of BJP MPs or Praveen Togadia, Muslims do not take it seriously because of their own existential daily experiences, the leaders of Hindu state do not inspire confidence among the Muslims. Christian minorities, Christian schools and Christian churches are targeted by emboldened Hindu organisations of the RSS. It is difficult for the besieged community to accept that the BJP government can act as their "protector". The upshot of the above description is that, Hindu-Muslim divide has become a reality. And if corrective step are not taken at the highest governmental and administrative levels, Indians will be living in a perpetual state of conflict and violence.

Peoples Democracy, April 5, 2015

11

Robber Capitalists of India

The CBI Special Court on April 9, 2015 sentenced Satyam Raju and his brother to spend seven years in jail for "forging documents and falsifying accounts in the country, in the biggest ever corporate accounting fraud" and on March 14, 2015 the CBI made arrests of a few government functionaries for stealing confidential documents for multi national consultancy firm, Price Water House Coopers and arrests of few others continued till the end of March for "Corporate Espionage". These two interrelated events could have been determined as routine aberrations of a few corporate houses; however, these two events of corporate fraud cannot be determined as routine because many "illegalities" are committed everyday by the capitalist class and global transnational monopoly capitalists around the world to 'maximise their profits' where means do not matter for the accumulators.

Americans have given the nomenclature of 'Lobbies and lobbying" on behalf of the monopolists in the corridors of State power to influence decision making of the executive and legislative branches of the government in favour of capitalist class in general and individual monopoly capitalists who are engaged in particular industry or business or trade.

What is the rationale for powerful lobbies and lobbyists to function in the interests of the capitalists through their 'contacts' with public decision makers?

A very significant fact from contemporary situation may be mentioned to reveal the reality of capitalism's methods for profit maximisation. The BJP MP Shyam Chandra Gupta, a *beedi* business baron, has made it a point to be a member of the parliamentary committee which is looking into the imposition of some restrictions on 'tobacco citizens'. Gupta's annual turnover of *beedi* business is Rs. 200-225 crore per year and such a person is to decide in a parliamentary committee for rules controlling the sale of tobacco. Second, the Modi government has issued an ordinance on mines and minerals, and it was to be approved in March 2015 session of the parliament. Kalpatru Das, the Biju Janata Dal MP was a member of parliamentary committee on the Mining Bill. He runs a mineral transport business. The presence of BJD MP in the committee on mines bill acted as a facilitator through his party for Modi government to get parliamentary approval for Mines and Minerals (Development and Regulation) Bill and Coal Mines (Special Provisions) Bill approved on March 20, 2015. The practise of elected MP's functioning as lobbyists and for the capitalists with whom their own business interests are linked is quite common in India because every kind of influence has to be exercised on public policy makers to get every kind of concession for profit seekers.

Arun Jaitly, the Indian finance minister, in response to growing public anger on misdeeds of capitalists, foreign multinationals 'thundered' on April 6, 2015 that India is not a 'tax haven'. Is India not a 'tax haven' for the mighty and influential capitalist class? It is well known and a documented fact that the big business houses employ all tricks to laws like income tax, customs, excise, banking etal and 'fudge' the accounts so that Indian monopolists declare themselves as 'No Tax Companies'. Arun Jaitley must be ruing his own assertion of April 6, that India was not a 'tax haven' because on April 10, a forensic report prepared for the Special Fraud Investigation Office (SFIO) reported that "over a third of India's top 500 companies including those in the top 100" are 'managing their accounts'. The upshot of evidence and facts is that the robber capitalists of India like all members of their global fraternity adopt every and any method, fair or foul, to maximise their profits and that their business empire can expand.

Ordinary citizens can be landed up in jail for breaking any law of the State, but the monopoly capitalists along with their global allies are able to 'cheat' the State and the State functionaries whether political executive or permanent professional bureaucrats. Is the government – of, by, and for the people, ignorant about basic reality of society? The forbes list of billionaires and global watch list of wealth of 2013-2014 shows that 'the wealth of 85 tycoons equals poorest half of humanity'. The super billionaires had earned US$ 686 per day (about Rs. 4000 crore) till March 2014.

India as a capitalist country is not an exception to the general rule of capitalism that wealth gets concentrated in a few hands only and absolute 'inequality' in society is fundamental to all capitalist societies.

Indian capitalism has grown and come of age with the support of its 'own ally' the Indian State which has formed an alliance with global capitalist State systems. Veerappa

Moily, former petroleum minister in the Manmohan Singh government publically admitted that 'he fek threatened by Indian oil import lobby' who did not want to make India a little self-reliant on the basis of domestic exploration of oil and gas. The capitalist class thrives and enjoys power and privileges for free accumulation of profits because the owners of private property for production of goods and services are protected by the State. It is one Satyam Raju or one Cairn India or one powerful transnational corporation which may be in the news for methods employed for accumulation. However, the reality is as shown above that the political economy of capitalist State of India has through its own logic provided opportunities and spaces for capitalists, individuals or groups, indigenous or foreign to accumulate, accumulate and accumulate with the generosity of its own instrument of the State in India.

People's Democracy, May 11-17, 2015

12

Govermentalization of Yoga

A Purely individual physical exercise like yoga has for the first time in the history of post-Independence India been given a national status because the central government announced that June 21 would become a landmark in Indian history when "the whole of India" would be officially expected to perform yoga exercises. The central government had asked every public servant, autonomous universities/ colleges and others to observe June 21 as International Yoga Day, which was accepted by the United Nations at the sole initiative of Prime Minister Narendra Modi. Further, it deserves to be clearly stated that for Yoga Day celebrations, a very large-scale mobilisation had been undertaken by all public institutions and private organisations, led by the Rashtriya Swayamsevak Sangh (RSS), and thousands of Hindu saints, sadhus and yoga teachers. It is also for the first time in the history of post-Independence India that the central government-led and announced programme on June 21 has been jointly undertaken by the government, the RSS, and Hindu yoga teachers, saints, sadhus and priestly clans.

The first analytical question which needs to be examined critically is that the "rationale" behind this programme of yoga, which in public eye is associated with Hindu mythological gods and scriptures. The government had to announce that 'surya namaskar' at the time of beginning of yoga exercise will not be "compulsory" because a very important section of the Muslim community had protested against this Hindu religious recitation. The issue does not end here. Indian people associate yoga with Hinduism and this public perception has been further solidified and strengthened by the decision of the central government because the ruling BJP is a Hindutva-vadi party and it is a political outfit of the Hindutva RSS, for which this country is inhabited by Hindu religious population.

How can a government at the centre and in the states led by a Hindutva-vadi party like BJP be disassociated from Hinduism of yoga? Can there be an iota of doubt in public mind about the Hinduism of yoga when Hindu yogis and RSS followers are actively and aggressively mobilising Hindus of India to observe June 21 as Yoga Day? Hindu scriptures have been quoted and mythological Hindu god has been identified as the first yoga creator? Lord Shiva is 'Adi-Yogi', or the first yogi. The story does not end here. Is the government of India and BJP governments in some of the major states are not aware that yoga teachers or gurus have commercialised yoga for private profits? The well honoured "businessman" of this trade is yoga guru Ramdev who as chief protagonist of 'yoga vidya' has been patronised by BJP in the government. The BJP-led Haryana government has made Ramdev some kind of special guru and the BJP government at the centre has publicly patronised him. Is the government not aware that an ill-educated and ill-trained Ramdev, the public face of yoga, is owner of so-called indigenously produced medicines at Haridwar? Is the government collaborating with thousands of yoga teachers, saints and sadhus who have made it a "profitable business" by manipulating the insecure and anxiety-ridden, vulnerable and extremely gullible Hindu masses? A fundamental issue of great public concern is that an elected prime minister, chief ministers and ministers in their official "public" position cannot be seen to be associated and partnering with yogis, or saints or sadhus of religious community. The BJP and the affiliates of RSS led, controlled and guided Hindu organisations through its public activities. The latest being the celebration of Yoga Day on June 21 publicly placed beyond any shadow of doubt that its every action is dedicated to achieve only one goal i.e. to establish Hindu Rashtra in which Hindu religious preachers have to occupy a place of pride. This is the agenda of the Sangh Parivaar and its political outfit, the BJP on whose band wagon businessmen like Ramdev or the whole parasitical Hindu priestly clan feels protected and promoted. The messenger's message is important and clear message is that the only protector of Hindu religion, its tradition, its rituals, its beliefs in India is the Sangh Parivaar and BJP, if it is in power. If the Hindus of India elect the BJP, they should feel assured that their rituals, beliefs, holy cow and holy temples, and their priests will be defended, otherwise the "believers" of foreign origin religions like Islam and Christianity living in India will have an upper hand over Hindus. Hindu practice of Saraswati Puja in schools and 'Surya Namashkar' et. all would be made compulsory to inculcate Hindu values to make better Hindus in Hindu India.

Hence, Yoga Day celebrations on June 21 as commanded from above can be seen as an integral part of Hinduisation of India as the goal of the Hindutvavadi BJP's government and Hindutva organisations including saints and sadhus. The real objection is that the government instead of performing its own duties in the field of promoting facilities in public health and public education, it is handing over its own basic activities to swamis, saints, yogis who are according to BJP and RSS are solely equipped to teach Hindu values based on Hindu rituals. The real significance of the BJP sponsored Yoga Day observation on June 21 can be only understood if this "decision" of the government is linked with the larger agenda of the BJP and the Sangh Parivaar of the 'Hindu Rashtravaad' because as one day event if looked in isolation from the whole agenda of Hinduisation of society and culture as interpreted by official government interpreters and Hindu sadhus and yogis then its real message is trivialised. Yogi Adityanath or Sakshi Maharaj as BJP MPs are not just individuals their activities and pronouncements against "religious minority communities" or Mohan Bhagwat and Home Minister Rajnath Singh's public pronouncement for the need for "rewriting and correction of Indian History textbooks" or government funded cultural and educational organisation engaged in the "rewriting or re-imagining of Indian Cultural History" to make people understand the greatness of 'Hindu India' are part of the total ideological agenda of the Sangh Parivaar and BJP and hence Yoga Day the great importance to yogis and priests attended by the Modi government are all inter-related and inter-connected.

The sum and substance of the above narrative is that Yoga Day observation or patronising of Ramdev and thousands of others yoga teachers, irrespective of the fact that even if they are engaged in shady business activities are all under the umbrella of BJP government and RSS as joint workers for the promotion of the cause of

Hinduisation of Indian Society as defined by politicians of the Sangh Parivaar. It is a political agenda and it is not the means but the end that matters. It is not only the Modi-led government and bureaucracy hyperactive in using the media to mobilise participants for Yoga Day. Modi himself an expert in sending Twitter messages, wrote on his Twitter page to "learn about Salabhasana or the locust pose and its positive effects for Yoga Day." He further continued "the posture improves flexibility in the back and improves digestion." The question thus occurs, why this Hinduisation of physical exercises, Mr. Modi? Why are Hindu outfits like RSS openly championing and actively promoting Yoga day?

13

Narendra Modi: The Chief of Misgovernance

On May 26, 2014, Narendra Modi had shouted from the rooftops that he believed in "minimum government and maximum governance". He had also boasted that unlike the Manmohan Singh-led UPA government which had been involved in deep acts of corruption in public life, he would provide a clean government because "he would himself be above corruption and he would not tolerate any act of corruption by his government functionaries." Arun Jaitley not to be left behind, spoke in his master's voice that the BJP would ensure probity in public life". The BJP propaganda machine went overtime by spreading a message among the voters that "Modi is clean, and strong" while "Manmohan was clean and weak" and hence the UPA government led by Manmohan could indulge in loot of public resources. These tall claims of 'Modi model of governance' have collapsed like a pack of cards just after completion of one year of Modi in-government

First, Sushma Swaraj, the Minister of External Affairs, helped Lalit Modi, a fugitive and absconder. A few salient features of Sushma Swaraj-Lalit Modi "inappropriate" dealings may be mentioned to substantiate the argument that it is for the first time in the history of post-independence India that an external affairs minister has brought a national disgrace by using the authority of her office to help a criminal who has escaped from the clutches of the investigating and prosecuting agencies of the country. This task was performed by the external affairs minister and the dealing with the functionaries of British government was done without consulting and informing anyone including the bureaucracy of her own ministry. Swaraj as the external affairs minister had facilitated the procurement of documents by Lalit Modi because "she herself and her husband and her daughter" have close family and professional relations with Modi and in the process "public and private" actions of the cabinet minister ceased to matter at all with the minister. The 'doctrine of conflict of interest' and "impropriety" on the part of the minister to help a family friend, a criminal, were all thrown in the wind.

Prime Minister Modi has to explain the misconduct of such a grave nature by his cabinet minister. A so called "strong" prime minister should have known about the alleged acts of omission and commission of his colleague. Modi's phoney claim of "strong prime minister" was meant to be an empty rhetoric for public consumption. Modi has to explain to the whole country about his own lapses while performing the duties of prime minister under whose leadership the external affairs minister had indulged in gross act of impropriety by "secretly" influencing the British government to extend favour to her 'family friend'. The story of Modi's incapacity to govern with probity and BJP's failure to maintain highest levels of honesty in public life do not end with Sushma. Vasundhara Raje, BJP chief minister of Rajasthan, while in London, as a guest of Lalit Modi, "was a witness in favour of Lalit Modi's immigration case". Vasundhara "signed an affidavit" which was required by the British Authorities to grant immigration to Lalit Modi, Vasundhara like Sushma did acts of extremely doubtful arid immoral character by ensuring that "Indian public should not know anything about it".

Hot Pursuit

It is a well-known saying that "secrecy" is always maintained to perform an act of "sin" or cross the boundaries of law and propriety. If on one hand, BJP and Modi in government, have been caught for serious acts of misuse and abuse of power, on the other, the Modi government undertook a highly secretive "military operation" into Myanmar, a neighbouring country, on a 'hot pursuit' to confront well-equipped armed insurgents who were hiding in Myanmar after committing acts of violence against Indian security forces in North-East India. Such exceptional and extraordinary acts of hot pursuit are undertaken by defence forces after informal parleys between the government of India and the country concerned. However, the BJP propaganda machine and BJP ministers at the centre went out of their way to publicly proclaim that Modi unlike the previous Congress-led UPA government, practiced 'hard' and not 'soft' policy while defending the nation's territorial interests. One minister of the Modi government thought it wise to tell Pakistan that India can repeat its Myanmar act in that country while dealing with "terrorist camps" in Pakistan. Pakistan, on expected lines, reacted very promptly and strongly. The defence forces of India also quietly protested against public celebrations by BJP and Modi's ministers on a highly sensitive military operation.

The manner in which the Modi government handled the issue of "hot pursuit" into Myanmar clearly shows complete incompetence of Modi as prime minister and has exposed his capacities to pursue a sober and well thought-out foreign policy of India. The upshot of above analytical narrative is that irrespective of the fact that whether these "two government functionaries" continue, in office or are forced to resign, Modi and the BJP get fully exposed and all these moral claims have collapsed. Modi has been handed over power by the defeated Congress-led UPA on the promise that Modi is a "doer", a performer. But the way he has managed public affairs during the last one year in office clearly shows that his rhetoric is at variance with the 'reality as it has been clearly seen by the Indian public'. It is extremely doubtful that the country's defence, security and foreign policies can be pursued in the style of Modi's governance as shown by the above narrative based on the acts of omission and commission in the field of foreign policy and defence and security pursued by Sushma Swaraj, Vasundhara Raje and the prime minister himself who completely mishandled the army's hot pursuit into Myanmar's territories.

The story does not end here. If BJP, Sangh Parivaar and Prime Minister Modi are unfit to govern a complex modern state of India, they are all successfully pursuing their basic agenda of 'Hinduisation' and 'polarisation' of society and the Modi government is pursuing the Hindutva programme with extra energy and commitment. The best illustration of such a facet of a Hindutvavadi party's governance programme has been publicly exposed by the special public prosecutor in the Malegaon blast case Rohini Salian on June 25, 2015. The ongoing trial of violent Hindu extremists involved to Malegaon blast killing.

People Democracy, July 6-12, 2015

14

A Year of Opposition

If on one hand, the Modi government is celebrating its one year in office at the centre beginning from May 26, 2014 to May 26, 2015, on the other hand, fragmented multiple opposition parties have once again recovered from the shock of its defeat when the Lok Sabha elections results were announced. On May 16, 2014 the BJP and the Sangh Parivar celebrated its extraordinary electoral victory in the Lok Sabha elections because it obtained 282 out of 543 seats on its own and with a majority of its own, it proclaimed from the house top that it will fulfill its agenda of "Minimum Government and Maximum Governance" and prove its credentials to put India on high growth road. The opposition parties like the All India Congress and the majority of regional and sub-regional parties were completed decimated before the unprecedented victory of BJP. The All-India Congress in its history of 67 years of post-independence got for the first time just ten per cent of Lok Sabha seats along with Mulayam Singh Yadav or Lalu Prasad or Sharad Yadav or Nitesh Kumar all of these stalwarts had been reduced to dust. The humiliation of opposition parties did not end here, because the State Assembly elections held in 2014 for Haryana, Maharashtra and Jharkhand, the BJP won the elections and formed its own government. The march forward of Narendra Modi seemed to be unstoppable because of BJP's electoral victory in the year 2014 and the impossible happened when in 2015 the BJP suffered a humiliating electoral defeat in Delhi when it got only three seats out of 70 in the Assembly elections. The unpredicted electoral victory of Aam Aadmi Party in 2015 along with slow revival of self-confidence among opposition parties and groups created a situation where opposition parties began an effective offensive against the acts of omission and commission of the Modi government. The Modi government took an unusual step of proclaiming ordinances to implement its some policies without going through the normal procedure of Parliamentary decisions and approval.

It deserves to be clearly stated that in a parliamentary system based on competitive multi-polar and multi-party democracy like that of India, opposition parties are a legitimate factor, even a pillar, which can hold a majority party government accountable and answerable. A few important events may be mentioned here which made the Modi government conscious of this fact that 'opposition parties' are alive and kicking, and these scattered groups can come on a 'common platform' to show their disapproval both in public and Parliament against Modi's style and substance of managing the government especially through Ordinances. First, Sonia Gandhi, the most acceptable face of the opposition parties and groups organized and led a powerful delegation of all opposition leaders to President to protest against politics of Ordinances of the Modi government. It must be clearly understood that the device and mechanism of using Ordinance in a parliamentary democracy is considered quite 'undesirable and if need arises this action is taken by a government under extremely exceptional circumstances. However, the Modi government made the habit of issuing Ordinances to overcome Parliamentary Opposition and this undemocratic short-cut brought the opposition on the streets of Delhi. Hence, the undemocratic style of rule of Ordinances provided an opportunity to make opposition parts active both in two Houses of Parliament and also on the streets. Opposition politics a necessary constituent of democracy got revived after its initial paralysis because of a shock of stunning election defeat in May 2014. Second, the opposition parties could not checkmate the unwanted legislation brought by the Modi government specially because some of the regional parties, as always, did not agree to unite together against the government, the opposition found a great opportunity to effectively criticize, oppose and delay government bills especially in the Rajya Sabha where the BJP was in a minority and opposition parties used there Rajya Sabha space with great advantage. Third, it should not be forgotten that opposition parties consist of very experienced leaders in both the Houses of Parliament like Sonia Gandhi, Mulayam Singh Yadav, Sharad Yadav, Mayawati et al who led their opposition from the front and effectively cornered the government on many occasions. Forth, the opposition got united on two very important issues which are very close to the Modi government like the Land Acquisition Bill and Goods and Services Bill. If Modi took the route of Ordinance to deal with Land Acquisition Bill, the Congress party in opposition, took the Land Acquisition Bill to the streets and on the floor of two Houses of Parliament, and alongwith other opposition parties, Congress led by Sonia Gandhi and reactivated and re-energized Rahul Gandhi in

2015 led demonstrations of farmers in difference places and successfully projected that the Modi's Government was "anti-farmer" and "pro-private capitalist" and this is the reason that it is acquiring farmers' land to hand it over to the rich capitalist. Farmers were brought on the road by the Congress. The communists and others to oppose the Land Acquisition by the Modi government and this activity of the opposition parties made them extremely active and relevant. The voices of farmers' against land acquisition were raised in Parliament and Opposition, especially Rahul Gandhi, in Lok Sabha and farmers champions like the CPI(M) and Janata Dal (United) et al in the Rajya Sabha where opposition, if united is in majority, compelled the government inspite of its reluctance, to refer the Land Acquisition Bill to Parliamentary Select Committee for deep consideration. It has been a big setback for the Modi government because it is committed to the big industrialists to transfer them land for setting up their factories. The Modi government is on the defensive and to refute opposition charge, the government and the Sangh Parivar is going out of the way to prove that it is "pro-poor and pro-farmer" and it is not pro-rich as successfully depicted by opposition parties. This is the first land mark in Indian democracy where inspite of 282 out 543 seats in the Lok Sabha, the BJP government has been compelled to reckon with the opposition parties which were completely ignored with contempt by BJP from May 26 to the end of 2014. The same story has been repeated on Goods and Services Tax which because of opposition's firm stand, has been referred to the Select Committee. The upshot of above narrative is clear that euphoria of electoral victory has come to an end and the BJP is now confronted with the reality democratic politics that it cannot aggressively walk roughly over the Opposition parties and it has to respect criticism and dissent of opposition and social groups which are supporters of opposition parties. The BJP-in-government during its first year in office has been compelled to come down on earth from its high spirits of victory and confront opposition parties, farmers and trade unions. The BJP-in-government in May 2015 is forced with the reality of democratic politics which is based on debate, dissent, opposition and not highhandedness of government by Ordinances.

Index